Mediterranean Diet Cookbook

40 Delicious, Healthy, and Easy-to-Make Mediterranean Diet Recipes!

By: Aubrey Mitchell

Disclaimer

This book provides the reader with a better understanding of the diet in hopes of making a difference in the reader's life, and also provides recipes.

The author of this book is not affiliated with any medical company, nor does the author provide medical treatment advice in any way. The ideas, views, and opinions expressed in this book are those of the author. The author assumes no liability for advice or suggestions offered in this book. The author and publisher of this book and the accompanying materials have used their best efforts in preparing this book. The author and publisher make no representation or warranties with respect to the accuracy, applicability, fitness, or completeness of the contents of this book. The information contained in this book is strictly for informational purposes. Therefore, if you wish to apply ideas contained in this book, you are taking full responsibility for your actions.

Mediterranean Diet Cookbook: 40 Delicious, Health, and Easy-to-Make Mediterranean Diet Recipes
Copyright © 2014 by Aubrey Mitchell. All rights reserved. No part of this book may be

reproduced in any form without permission in writing from the author.

Table of Contents

Disclaimer 2
What is the Mediterranean Diet? 7
The Benefits of Eating Mediterranean Diet 12
Some Tips on How to Master Mediterranean Cooking 14
40 Awesome Mediterranean Diet Recipes 19
   Pasta with Basil–Based Sauce 20
   Pita Sandwiches Stuffed with Greek Salad ... 22

   22
   Sicilian-Style Cauliflower Salad 24
   Greek Salad 26
   Grilled Salmon 29
   Mediterranean-Style Quinoa Salad 31
   Mediterranean-Style Panini 34
   Griddled Chicken 36

Walnut Granola Cereals 38

Balsamic Chicken and Mediterranean Salad 40

Greek Salad with Orzo and Black-Eyed Peas
.... 43

Mediterranean Kale Salad with Roasted Grape
Vinaigrette 46

Mint-Flavored Grilled Lamb Chops 50

Roasted Mediterranean vegetables and
polenta 52

Chicken and Penne 54

Classic Pasta Salad 57

Potato salad, Mediterranean-Style 59

Couscous with Oil-Cured Olives 62

Roasted Vegetables in Balsamic Sauce 64

Artichokes Provencal 67

Tuscan-style white bean stew 69

Chorizo pilaf 74

Homemade Vegetable Pizza 77

Zucchini "Tagliatelle" 81

Spicy Escarole 83

Eggplant with Yogurt and Dill 85

Braised Kale 87

"For Adults Only" Mediterranean Chicken 89

Tuna Salad Supreme 93

Broccoli Rabe 95

Classic Caponata 97

Roasted Eggplant & Walnut Dip 102

Shrimp Skewers with Tzatziki and Feta Cheese 105

Bulgur Salad 107

Poached Pear in Orange and Apple Juice .. 110

Avocado and Tuna Tapas 112

Mediterranean-Style Chickpea Patties 115

Chili Spinach Salad 117

Mediterranean-style scones 120

Mediterranean Veggie Wrap 122

A Sample 7-Day Mediterranean Diet for Transitioning into Healthy Eating 125

Conclusion 127

What is the Mediterranean Diet?

If you got this book because you want to cook healthy Mediterranean recipes to move your Mediterranean diet along, chances are that you already know far more about the Mediterranean Diet that you no longer need a concise answer to this question. If you are in that boat, then no worries; this book primarily focuses on giving you 40 awesome and healthy recipes that you can cook at any time of the day in order to fuel your drive for a healthier and more fulfilling diet.

However, if you have little inkling as to what the Mediterranean diet can offer in terms of health benefits, then fear not! In the succeeding paragraphs, we'll touch briefly about the Mediterranean diet, what it is about, a little bit of the history, before diving into the 40 awesome recipes that can help transform the way you look at eating. Now, if that's still not enough, we recommend that you pick up the accompanying ebook entitled "The Mediterranean Diet: Modern Healthy Eating and What It Can Do for You." That book talks about the Mediterranean diet in more detail, diving into the nitty-gritty of what makes this diet THE diet of choice today. You will also find a few basic recipes in there as well as a comprehensive shopping and grocery guide that will help you stock your shelves more effectively when transitioning to Mediterranean eating.

So now that we've gotten those out of the way, let's go back to the first question we asked: what is the Mediterranean diet and what benefits can one expect when transitioning into Mediterranean style eating?

In simplest terms, the Mediterranean diet is a modern adaptation of the diet of the people living around the Mediterranean Sea. Modern studies have shown that people around the Mediterranean have a longer lifespan compared to people in other locations around the world. In addition, the incidence of serious and potential illnesses around this area is also markedly lower than in other areas around the globe. Doctors, dieticians, researchers and other experts theorized that diet plays a major role in explaining the relatively better health surrounding the Mediterranean Sea and this led to the creation of the Mediterrancan Diet as a concept that is quickly gaining attraction today.

The graphic below conveniently summarizes the essential points of the Mediterranean diet from ingredients of great importance at the bottom of the pyramid to ingredients that are not preferred located at the top.

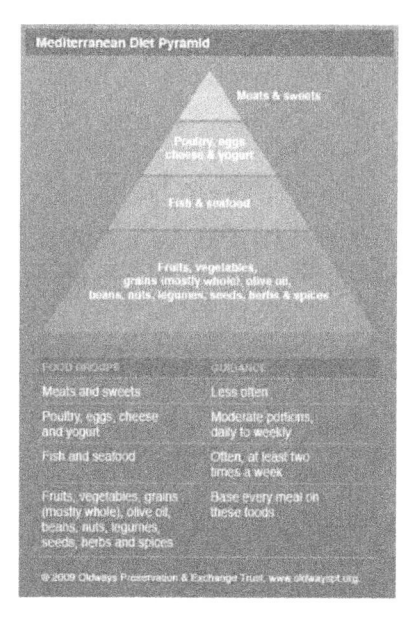

Source: The Mayo Clinic

Some of the most notable features of the Mediterranean diet include the following:

- The Mediterranean diet advocates the use of olive oil is the preferred source of fat. Other sources of fat such as in animal meat like read meat are cut to a minimum.

- The diet strongly advocates increasing one's intake of fresh, seasonal fruits and vegetables. In many recipes, the fruits and vegetables actually become the star of the dish while the lean meats become the garnish.

- People around the Mediterranean Sea love their bread and their pasta. This is largely replicated in the modern Mediterranean diet but with a few tweaks including emphasis on whole grain flour as opposed to the conventional wheat-based flour.

- Red wine is a staple particularly in Mediterranean dinners. While this cookbook does not include the profuse

use of red wine as a cooking ingredient, the use of red wine during the meal itself is actually already assumed a given.

- Spices play a big role in Mediterranean cooking, particularly the spices that are common to the area. If you've watched a lot of Italian and Greek cooking shows for example, you would have already known that spices like basil, mint, oregano, and rosemary, together with lemon and garlic flavors are used quite commonly and in generous amounts. Expect the same approach here.

The specific tenets of the Mediterranean Diet, therefore, gives rise to a few notable traits that should help you decide if the Mediterranean is aligned with your health and wellness goals. First, heavy use of bread and pasta means the Mediterranean Diet isn't for those eyeing a low-carb meal. The use of fresh ingredients also means you need to be modestly proficient in the kitchen, and this cookbook is specifically written to show you the way. Mediterranean diet meals also tend to be served in smaller portions so this isn't for someone eyeing heavy and filling meals. If you're a meat lover, this diet is also not compatible with your meat cravings.

In essence, that's all it! The Mediterranean Diet is a simple but effective way to help you meet your health goals by focusing more on fresh fruit and vegetable ingredients. It also promotes a deeper appreciation of the way food is prepared as one would do in a small village in Italy overlooking the Mediterranean (the Amalfi Coast and Sicily come to mind).

If you are mindful of these considerations, then you are ready to take on the challenge of trying out these awesome healthy recipes that we put together to help you ease into the Mediterranean habit.

But first, let's quickly talk about the benefits of eating, Mediterranean style.

The Benefits of Eating Mediterranean Diet

The main benefit with the Mediterranean diet is lowering one's risk towards heart ailments. In fact, the core research that formed the basis of the modern Mediterranean dieting philosophy was based on comparing heart disease rates between people living around the Mediterranean Sea to other cultures around the world. At first, one of the conclusions was that the relatively heavy use of red wine by the French and the Italians helped to explain the markedly lower incidence of heart disease in the area. However, it quickly became apparent that a more holistic reason resided in the diet of Mediterranean cultures and not just from the wine drinking. Hence, embracing Mediterranean-style meals on a regular basis should lower one's risk factors for heart disease.

In addition, there is also correlative evidence that helps support the benefits of the diet in other areas of health. The high antioxidant and bioflavonoid levels common in the Mediterranean diet lead to better resistance against inflammatory diseases like arthritis and gout. There are also medical studies that correlate increased bioflavonoids intake to a reduction in the risk factors for various types of cancer.

The holistic and balanced nutrition coming from plant-based diets as in the case of the Mediterranean diet also helps in reducing one's risks for diabetes, hypertension, high bad cholesterol levels, as well as in mitigating lifestyle factors that can lead to Alzheimer's and Parkinson's disease.

And then, there's everyone's favorite buzzword these days: weight loss!

If you want to know more about the benefits of the Mediterranean diet, pick-up the accompanying ebook to this cookbook as we've already mentioned in the introduction.

Some Tips on How to Master Mediterranean Cooking

Unfortunately, one of the most serious obstacles to healthy eating for many of us is our limited skills in the kitchen. Let's face it, between the shopping, the preparation, the techniques, and our general fear of messing up whatever is on the stove, diets that require some wee-bit of culinary wizardry can leave some of us grasping for straws.

So the first thing one has to realize is that learning how to cook Mediterranean dishes does not require a PhD in the culinary sciences. On the contrary, Mediterranean recipes emphasize a bare-bones approach to cooking; that is, if cooking can be avoided as in the case of salads, thereby preserving the freshness of the ingredients, then so be it. If not, then you allow the ingredients to simply speak for themselves by virtue of their freshness and natural flavors. In short, you don't need to learn any new fancy cooking technique to be able to prepare great healthy dishes such as the ones in this cookbook.

But just so that we cover our bases, here are some useful tips that you can employ to master Mediterranean cooking. These tips are not set in stone but when you feel that you are lost, you can always go back to these tips in preparing the recipes here or in any other cookbook or website that talks about the Mediterranean diet.

1. Do not every try to overcook your ingredients. With fresh ingredients, you are much better off undercooking than

overcooking ingredients. Overcooking destroys the natural nutrients in the food and ruins the flavor of the dish. If you don't know how to judge if ingredients are already cooked or not, stay on the safe side by preferring the ingredients to be a bit undercooked leaving them with a lot of crunch.
2. Always cook hard ingredients first and then gradually add in the soft ingredients and lastly, the leafy greens. Between carrots and tomatoes, for example, the carrots go in first before the tomatoes.
3. Olive oil is a staple in Mediterranean cooking. If you've watched a few Italian cooking shows, you might have noticed that olive oil is used in almost all recipes. You can also pick up that habit to add more flavor and nutrition to every Mediterranean recipe. If you must pick up one cliché, it is that everything is better with olive oil.
4. Avoid cooking in high heat. Heat destroys the ingredients and increases the risks for overcooking. Cook in medium to low heat

where you have more control of the cooking process. As a simple example, smoking oil in a hot pan indicates that the oil is too hot. That's bad for cooking for the reasons that we've already talked about, so learn to turn the heat down for more flavorful dishes that retain their nutrient content.
5. The only exception to cooking in high heat is when you're cooking in water. With water in a pot, you can always turn the heat up until the water boils, then turn it down again to allow it to simmer as you add ingredients.
6. When sautéing with olive oil, the only rule is to make sure that ingredients do not burn. For this, you only need to constantly toss the ingredients for about 30 seconds before adding the main ingredients.
7. The amount of ingredients indicated in Mediterranean recipes is only a guide and not a hard rule. Feel free to add or subtract ingredients as you like. Of course, it you are really new to cooking, you can always be to-the-point when you

start. As you gain more experience, you can begin experimenting with amounts and quantities to get the taste you want. Unless…
8. You are baking, in which case ingredient sizes need to be really exact.

If you plan to try more complex recipes, and then aren't a lot of them in Mediterranean cooking, you can always choose to watch videos online, or better yet enroll in a culinary class that focuses on Mediterranean cooking. With the popularity of this diet, it's virtually guaranteed that there's a class in a city near you.

That's it. Now that you're ready, let's jump straight into the 40 awesome healthy recipes we specifically prepared to help you get started with your Mediterranean diet.

40 Awesome Mediterranean Diet Recipes

Here are the 40 recipes that we feel best represent Mediterranean cooking. All of these recipes are chosen because of their simplicity but also because we wanted to be diverse enough to showcase different ingredients that are common in Mediterranean cooking. The recipes speak for themselves so check the directions and you should be able to prepare a kick-ass healthy dish with ease.

And as always, enjoy the process! The cooking and food preparation should be just as fun as the eating itself!

Pasta with Basil-Based Sauce

The pasta is fairly straight-forward and you have undoubtedly cooked many types of pasta over the years. The basil-based sauce is the tricky part in this recipe but it's not too complicated that you shouldn't be able to make it regardless of your proficiency level in the kitchen. As a nice aside, the basil-based sauce works for many other recipes such as a dip for raw veggies or even as a topping on your next pizza.

Image credit: Getty Images

Yield: 4 servings

Best Served For: Dinner

Ingredients:

- 1 pinch salt
- 1 pound linguine
- water (for cooking the pasta)

- 1 cup basil leaves
- 1 cup flat leaf parsley
- 1 cup olives, pitted
- 2 medium cloves of garlic
- 1 tbsp. fresh lemon juice
- 4 tbsp. extra-virgin olive oil
- ½ cup parmesan cheese, freshly grated

Directions:

1. In a large pot, add water, salt, and a little bit of oil. Put into high heat until it boils. While waiting for the water to boil, wash and clean the basil and parsley. If you have a blender or food processor available, use this to blend or process the basil and parsley. If not, you can finely chop the leaves, then mix in the garlic, olives, and lemon juice until smooth and thick.
2. When the water boils, toss in the pasta to cook. Once done, drain the water from the pasta and then toss it into a large bowl together with the basil-based sauce. Add more olive oil and cheese to flavor.
3. This recipe is best served hot.

Nutrition Facts:

Total Calories: 375, 214mg sodium, 59g carbs, 4g fiber, 10g polyunsaturated fat, 1g saturated fat, 2g sugar, 11g protein, 59mg calcium, 3mg iron.

Pita Sandwiches Stuffed with Greek Salad

You already know that breads are fairly common in the Mediterranean diet but breads, by themselves, tend to quickly become boring and bland. The addition of the Greek salad stuffing elevates this recipe to the next level.

To make the recipe that much simpler, you can always buy pita sandwiches from your favorite local bakery and work on the salads so you can quickly prepare a simple but healthy and very filling meal that works either as a light lunch or a heavy snack.

Image credit: Tina Rupp

Serving Size: 4 servings

Best Served For: Breakfast, lunch, afternoon snacks

Ingredients:

- 3 tbsp. extra-virgin olive oil
- 1 tbsp. red wine vinegar
- 1 ¼ cups cherry tomatoes, chopped, seeded
- 1 cup cucumber, chopped, seeded
- 1 cup green bell pepper, chopped
- 2/3 cup red onion, chopped
- ½ cup radishes, chopped
- ½ cup fresh parsley, chopped
- 1 cup crumbled feta cheese
- 4 8-in (dia) whole wheat pita breads, halved

Directions:

1. Mix all the salad ingredients together in a bowl. In a separate jar or bowl, mix together the olive oil and red wine vinegar and season with salt to taste.

2. If you want to use the salad later, you can prepare it up to 2 days ahead and allow to sit in the refrigerator. Only mix in the feta cheese when you are ready to serve.

3. To stuff sandwiches, spoon the salad into the bread and serve immediately.
4. Goat cheese can also be used if feta cheese is not available.

Nutrition Facts:

Total calories: 397, 20g total fat, 7g saturated fat, 33mg cholesterol, 775mg sodium, 45g carbs, 7g fiber, 13g protein.

Sicilian-Style Cauliflower Salad

You may not think of cauliflower as something you can pop into the oven to roast so this recipe will allow you to do just that. From there, you have the freedom to play around with the flavors you like. The resulting salad can then be used as a substitute for conventional carbs in any diet.

Image credit: Karen Pickus

Yield: 4 servings

Best Served For: Lunch, Dinner

Ingredients:

- 1 head cauliflower, cut into smaller pieces
- 8 tbsp. extra-virgin olive oil
- salt
- ½ cup raisins
- 1 cup wine
- 1 lemon, juiced, zest grated
- 1 orange, juiced, zest grated
- 1 tsp. white anchovy, minced
- 1 tsp. red pepper flakes
- 1 tsp. cumin seeds, toasted
- 1 tbsp. raw honey
- 4 shallots, minced
- 1 clove garlic, minced
- ½ cup pine nuts, toasted
- 2 tbsp. capers
- 2 tbsp. flat-leaf parsley, chopped

Directions:

1. In an oven preheated to 400°F, toss in the cauliflower together with salt and 2 tablespoons of olive oil. Toast for about 20 minutes.

2. While toasting the cauliflower, drop the raisins in the wine to soak in more flavor. After about 10 minutes, add the lemon orange juice, zest, anchovies, cumin, honey and red pepper flakes. Finish by adding 6 tablespoons olive oil and mix well. Once mixed, add the remaining ingredients – shallots, garlic, capers, and salt to taste.
3. Mix the roasted cauliflower and the vinaigrette and finish with finely chopped parsley.

Nutrition Facts:

Total calories: 425, 15g total fat, 3g saturated fat, 10mg cholesterol, 620mg sodium, 75g carbs, 9g fiber, 11g protein.

Greek Salad

This classic Greek salad is as simple as you can ever get with Mediterranean cooking. It is easy to prepare and takes advantage of the natural flavors of fresh ingredients making it one of the most sought after recipes for those who are only new to the Mediterranean diet.

Yield: 4 servings

Best Served For: Lunch, Dinner

Ingredients:

- 1 small red onion, chopped
- salt
- 2 cups iced water
- ¼ cup red wine vinegar
- 1 lemon, juiced, zest grated
- 1 tsp. raw honey
- 1 tsp. oregano
- pepper, freshly ground
- ½ cup extra-virgin olivo oil
- 12 small tomatoes, quartered
- 1 cup olives, halved, pitted
- 5 cucumbers, chopped
- ½ cup feta cheese (4-ounce block)

Image credit: Johnny Miller

Directions:

1. Prepare the ingredients. Soak the red onion in a bowl of salted iced water for about 15 minutes to eliminate the strong bitter taste. Peel and chop the cucumbers, and chop the tomatoes.

2. To prepare the dressing, mix the red wine vinegar with the lemon juice and zest, raw honey, and finish with salt and pepper to taste. Meanwhile, vigorously whisk or beat the olive oil until it emulsifies. To this, add the tomatoes and olives and toss until properly mixed.
3. Mix all the ingredients and toss properly to evenly distribute the flavors. Finish by slicing the feta cheese and adding into the top of the salad.

Nutrition Facts:

Total calories: 225, 19g total fat, 6g saturated fat, 4mg cholesterol, 440mg sodium, 45g carbs, 14g fiber, 10g protein.

Grilled Salmon

Salmon is one of the healthiest fish meats that you can ever find and is a staple in Moditerranean diet. It is rich in essential fatty acids Omega-3 and Omega-6 and has no cholesterol and unhealthy fats.

Image credit: Coastal Critters Lambakes and Grilling

Yield: 4 servings

Best Served For: Lunch, Dinner

Ingredients:

- 4 tbsp. fresh basil, chopped
- 1 tbsp. fresh parsley, chopped
- 1 tbsp. garlic, minced
- 2 tbsp. lemon juice
- 4 5-ounce salmon fillets
- black pepper, to taste
- salt

- 4 olives, chopped
- 4 thin slices lemon, to garnish

Directions

1. In a bowl, mix the parsley, basil, garlic and lemon juice. Rub the salmon fillets with salt and pepper and the basil-lemon juice mixture before putting the fillets on the grill. Make sure not to overcrowd the grill so the fish cooks properly. You can use any standard grill that you have or a broiler as an alternative.

2. Grill over high heat and turn when the edges of the fillet turn white. This should not take more than 5 minutes. Upon turning, put the fillet on a cooler portion of the grill to prevent overcooking. In the case of an electric or gas-fired grill, reduce the heat after turning the fish over. The fillet is cooked when it has turned opaque throughout.

3. Serve with green olives and lemon slices as garnish.

Nutrition Facts:

Total calories 183, sodium 105mg, total fat 9g, total carbs 2 g, saturated fat 1.5 g, fat (monounsaturated) 3g, protein 28 g, cholesterol 78 mg.

Mediterranean-Style Quinoa Salad

This is a simple and healthy salad that is easy to prepare and suitable for lunch or dinner.

Image credit: Allrecipes.com

Yield: 4 servings

Best Served For: Breakfast, lunch, dinner

Ingredients:

- 2 cups water
- 1 clove garlic, crushed
- 1 cup quinoa, uncooked
- 2 chicken breasts,

- boiled, chopped into small pieces
- 1 red onion, diced
- 1 green bell pepper, diced
- ½ cup olives, chopped
- ½ cup feta cheese
- ¼ cup fresh parsley, chopped
- ¼ cup fresh chives, chopped
- ½ tsp. salt
- 2/3 cup lemon juice
- 1 tbsp. balsamic vinegar
- ¼ cup olive oil

Directions:

1. Heat the water to a boil and add the garlic. After about 1 minute, add in the quinoa and reduce heat to simmer. It takes about 15 to 20 minutes for the quinoa to completely cook through. Once cooked, scoop out the garlic.
2. Take out the quinoa and in a bowl, add the remaining ingredients. Allow the dish to cool down for a few minutes before serving.

Nutrition Facts:

Total calories: 175, 12g total fat, 3g saturated fat, 0 mg cholesterol, 210mg sodium, 55g carbs, 12g fiber, 6g protein.

Mediterranean-Style Panini

Put a twist to the traditional sandwich by preparing this Mediterranean-style Panini instead. It's so easy to prepare and is ideal for breakfast or as an afternoon snack. You can also experiment with different types of bread to get the flavor that you want and to boost the nutritional value of the Panini.

Image credit: Health.com

Yield: 4 servings

Best Served For: Breakfast, Afternoon Snack

Ingredients:

- ½ cup mayonnaise dressing
- ¼ cup olive oil
- ¼ cup fresh basil, chopped
- 2 tbsp. black olives, finely chopped, preferably oil-cured
- 8 slices whole grain bread
- 1 small zucchini, thinly sliced
- 4 slices cheese (provolone or alternative)
- ¾ cup roasted red peppers, drained, sliced

Directions:

1. Combine the mayonnaise, olive oil, basil and olives in a bowl. Spread the dressing on to 4 slices of bread and top with zucchini, cheese, and peppers. Complete by topping with the remaining bread slices to form a sandwich.
2. Quickly cook the sandwiches on medium heat over a grill pan. You know that the Panini is ready when it turns golden

brown and the cheese has melted. Serve hot.

Nutrition Facts:

Total calories: 255, 18g total fat, 4g saturated fat, 0.3 mg cholesterol, 110mg sodium, 85g carbs, 16g fiber, 7g protein.

Griddled Chicken

This griddle chicken recipe is simple to make and perfect for dinner! Enjoy!

Image credit: Goodfood.com

Yield: 4 servings

Best Served For: Dinner

Ingredients:

- 225g quinoa, uncooked
- 1 25g stick butter

- 1 red chili, seeded, finely chopped
- 1 garlic clove, crushed
- 400g chicken fillets
- 1½ tbsp. extra-virgin olive oil
- water
- 200g vine tomatoes, chopped
- 10 pcs. black olives, pitted
- 1 red onion, sliced
- ½ cup feta cheese, crumbled
- 5 mint leaves, finely chopped
- ½ lemon, juiced, zest grated

Directions

1. In a pot, boil water in high heat. Once boiling, add the quinoa and reduce to medium heat to simmer. Cook for about 20 minutes until the quinoa is tender.

2. In a bowl, mix the butter, garlic and chili to create a light paste and set aside. Add 2 teaspoons of olive oil and seasoning into a hot griddle pan, then toss the chicken fillets for about 3 minutes on each side. Once thoroughly cooked, take out of the heat and dip in the spicy butter mix. Set aside for 3 minutes to allow the butter to melt.

3. In another bowl, mix the tomatoes, onion, feta cheese, mint and olives. Add the cooked quinoa and finish by dressing with lemon juice and lemon zest.
4. To serve, lay the quinoa salad first and finish by topping with the chicken fillets.

Nutrition Facts:

Total calories 473, protein 37g, carbs 35g, total fat 20g, saturated fat 8g, dietary fiber 2g, sugar 8g, salt 1.4g.

Walnut Granola Cereals

There are plenty of healthy Mediterranean diet breakfast recipes starting with this easy-to-prepare granola and walnut cereals. If you are in a hurry for work or an early-morning appointment, take some 10 minutes to prepare this filling and healthy meal to power you through the morning rush.

Image credit: Walnuts.org

Yield: 8 servings

Best Served For: Breakfast

Ingredients:

- 4 cups rolled oats (not instant)
- 2 cups natural wheat bran
- 1 ½ cups chopped walnuts
- ½ cups raw honey
- 2 tsp. vanilla essence
- 1 ½ cups raisins
- ½ cup dried fruits of your choice
- ¼ cup fresh fruit, chopped, for garnish (optional)

Directions:

1. Preheat your oven to 300°F. While heating, mix rolled oats, bran and walnuts in a bowl. In a separate microwaveable

bowl, mix the honey and vanilla essence and pop into the microwave for about 15 seconds or until the honey melts and runs thinly. Pour the honey-vanilla mixture into the dry ingredients and mix.
2. Spread the granola mixture over a baking pan lined with baking paper for about 30 minutes. The mixture is cooked with the granola turns golden brown.
3. Take out of the oven and set aside to cool. As the granola cools, add the raisins, dried fruits and fresh fruits to finish. This can last up to 2 weeks when stored in an airtight container.

Nutrition Facts:

Total calories: 460, total Fat 15g, saturated fat 2g, monounsaturated fat 3g, polyunsaturated fat 10g, cholesterol 0mg, sodium 7mg, carbs 81g, fiber 13g, protein 12g.

Balsamic Chicken and Mediterranean Salad

This is a complete carbs-and-protein dish that you can prepare for dinner. Make sure you choose the leanest part of the chicken to minimize your animal fat intake.

Yield: 6 servings

Best Served For: Dinner

Image credit: Getty Images

Ingredients:

- ¾ pound chicken breast, boneless, skinless
- 18 cherry tomatoes
- 1 medium zucchini
- 1 large yellow pepper, cored, seeded
- 9 small sweet onions, halved
- 3 tbsp. balsamic vinegar
- 1 tbsp. dijon mustard
- 4 tbsp. extra-virgin olive oil
- Six slices of whole-wheat bread loaf, lightly toasted
- 10 cups baby arugula leaves

- 2 cups fresh basil leaves
- 1 cup cooked chickpeas
- salt, black pepper

Directions:

1. Cut the chicken into 18 pieces in typical kebab-style sizes. Do the same for the sweet onion, zucchini, and yellow pepper. Use six metal skewers and into each, alternate the chicken, zucchini, tomato, pepper and onion together in whatever preferred order you like. Each skewer should have 3 of each component once done.
2. Before cooking, brush all the skewered ingredients with the balsamic vinegar. Cook on a grill in medium heat for about 10 minutes.
3. To serve, lay down arugula, basil, and chickpeas on plates as a salad base. Add the bread and one skewer. Drizzle each plate with the remaining vinaigrette to finish.

Nutrition Facts:

Total Calories: 498, 874mg sodium, 52g carbs, 10g dietary fiber, 3g saturated fat, 19g total fat, 13g sugars, 32g protein, 220mg calcium, 4mg iron.

Greek Salad with Orzo and Black-Eyed Peas

This easy-to-make recipe is also a staple of many vegetarian and vegan diets worldwide. However, despite the fact that this has been seen in various incarnations over the last few years, the recipe actually truly has its root in Mediterranean cuisine. Enjoy this salad as a light dinner or filling breakfast. The total preparation time is only about 15 minutes and is highly doable even on hectic mornings.

Yield: 4 servings

Best Served For: Breakfast, Light dinner

Image credit: Paul Grimes and Shelley Wiseman

Ingredients:

- ¾ cup orzo, uncooked
- 2 cups black-eyed peas
- 1 large tomato, diced
- 2 tbsp. flat-leaf parsley, chopped

- 2 tbsp. red-wine vinegar
- 1/3 cup red onion, finely sliced
- 2 tbsp. extra-virgin olive oil
- water
- pepper
- salt
- ½ cucumber, diced
- ½ cup olives, pitted
- 1 tsp. grated lemon zest
- 2 tbsp. fresh lemon juice
- 1 tbsp. oregano, finely chopped
- 2 cups romaine, chopped
- ½ pound feta cheese, crumbled
- 4 pcs. pepperoncini

Directions:

1. In a saucepan, add water, salt and oil and bring to a boil. Once boiling, add the orzo and cook for about 10 minutes until tender. Drain, cool, and set aside.
2. In a bowl, mix the black-eyed peas, parsley, and tomato and season with red wine vinegar, olive oil, salt, and pepper. Let the mixture sit for 15 minutes to allow the flavors to seep into the vegetables.
3. In a separate bowl, toss the orzo with olive oil, olives, lemon juice, zest, cucumber, onions, and flavor with salt and pepper.
4. Serve by layering as in the picture above with the black-eyed peas in the bottom following by the orzo, romaine and the feta on top. Garnish with pepperoncini and serve.

Nutrition Facts:

Total calories 365, protein 22g, carbs 48g, total fat 16g, saturated fat 3g, dietary fiber 8g, sugar 1 g, salt 3g.

Mediterranean Kale Salad with Roasted Grape Vinaigrette

As fat as Mediterranean salads go, this is one of the simplest but also one of the healthiest and a definite favorite for many. Go ahead and embrace the kale revolution with this tasteful and well-flavored take of a common healthy ingredient that's also fueling the global superfood revolution.

Image credit: Karen Pickus

Serving Size: 4 servings

Best Served For: Light lunch, light dinner

Ingredients:

- 1 cup red seedless grapes
- 2 tbsp. honey
- ¼ cup extra-virgin olive oil
- salt and pepper
- 2 tbsp. apple cider vinegar
- 1 tbsp. fresh lemon juice

- 2 green apples
- ½ cup extra-virgin olive oil, for drizzling
- 1 cup walnut, halved
- 1 cup kale
- 3 cups mixed winter greens (such as green and beet greens, chard, etc.)
- ½ cup goat cheese (or your preferred equivalent)

Directions:
1. To make the vinaigrette, preheat the oven to 450°F. Meanwhile, chop the grapes into small chunks leaving behind just a handful of whole ones. Toss the chopped grapes into a pan and mix with olive oil and honey. Season the mixture with salt to taste, then pop into the over for about 10 minutes until the skins blister. Remove from the oven and carefully transfer the roasted grape clusters to a plate and set aside.
2. Take out the grapes from the oven and allow to rest for about 5 minutes. Afterwards, pour apple cider vinegar, ¼ cup of olive oil and lemon juice. Sprinkle a dash of pepper then toss the remaining whole grapes into the pan. Mash the mixture together until you get the vinaigrette consistency that you want.
3. Core the apples, slice thinly, and arrange on a baking pan covered with baking sheet. Lightly drizzle olive oil and salt, add the walnuts by the side and roast together for about 15 minutes.
4. To prepare the salad, lay down the kale and other greens on a plate and top with

the roasted grapes, walnuts, apple and cheese. Drizzle with the vinaigrette to taste and serve.

Nutrition Facts:

Total calories 312, protein 28g, carbs 34g, total fat 24g, saturated fat 5g, dietary fiber 19g, sugar 0 g, salt 6g.

Mint-Flavored Grilled Lamb Chops

Meat may not be common in Mediterranean cooking but lamb has to be one of the more famous exceptions. Lamb meat is lean and full of protein that can help augment your protein intake when you are in the midst of a full-on Mediterranean diet with minimal meat dishes for days on end.

Yield: 6 servings

Best served for: Dinner

Image credit: Con Poulos

Ingredients:

- 1/3 cup extra-virgin olive oil
- ½ cup fresh mint leaves, chopped,
- ¼ tsp. red pepper flakes
- salt
- 12 small rib lamb chops
- 2 cloves garlic, smashed

Directions:

1. Preheat your grill to medium heat. In a bowl, mix the olive oil, red pepper flakes, mint, and salt to taste. Use the mixture as a rub for the lamb chops.
2. Grill the chops for about 4 minutes per side until the meat is slightly charred. Take out of the heat and brush the remaining mint oil on the lamb chops to finish.

Nutrition Facts:

Total calories 345, protein 65g, carbs 40g, total fat 28g, saturated fat 7g, dietary fiber 15g, sugar 0 g, salt 6g.

Roasted Mediterranean vegetables and polenta

Polenta is coarse corn grits that are common in Italian and Greek cuisines as a substitute for other forms of carbs. The resulting dish is simple and rustic that's packed with healthy goodness. This basic Mediterranean recipe can easily become a staple addition to your healthy eating habit.

Image credit: Israelikitchen.com

Yield: 6 servings

Best served for: Lunch, dinner

Ingredients:

- 1 small eggplant, peeled, cut
- 1 small yellow and 1 small green zucchini
- 6 medium mushrooms, sliced
- 6 sun-dried

- tomatoes, rehydrated
- 1 sweet red pepper, seeded
- 2 tbsp. extra-virgin olive oil
- 6 cups water
- 1 ½ cups coarse polenta
- 2 tsp. margarine
- ¼ tsp. black pepper
- 2 cups spinach
- 2 plum tomatoes, sliced
- 10 ripe olives, chopped
- 2 tsp. oregano

Directions:

1. Heat the grill and lift the rack about 4 inches above the heat source to regulate the rate of cooking of the vegetables.
2. Prior to grilling, brush with olive oil. Put on top of the grill and turn regularly to prevent the vegetables from charring. The vegetables are cooked when all sides are lightly browned. Remove from heat and
3. While the vegetables are cooking, heat water to a boil in a pan. When the water has boiled, add in the polenta, pepper and margarine to flavor. The polenta is cooked

when it has the same consistency as coarsely-mashed potatoes
4. To serve, lay down the polenta on a plate, add the spinach, tomatoes, olives and other toasted vegetables. Season with salt and pepper to serve.

Nutrition Facts:

Total calories 245, sodium 90 mg, total fat 7 g, carbs 39 g, saturated fat 2 g, dietary fiber 7 g, monounsaturated fat 4 g, protein 6 g, cholesterol 0 mg.

Chicken and Penne

This is a simple chicken and penne dish that's quite common in Italian cooking. To adopt it to a Mediterranean diet, always use boneless and skinless chicken so as to limit the fat in your diet.

Image credit: Allrecipe.com

Yield: 4 servings

Best served for: Dinner

Ingredients:

- 2 cups penne
- 1 ½ tbsp. butter
- ½ cup red onion, chopped
- 2 cloves garlic, minced
- 1 pound skinless, boneless chicken
- 1 ½ cup artichoke hearts
- 1 tomato, chopped
- ½ cup feta cheese, crumbled
- 3 tbsp. fresh parsley, chopped
- 2 tbsp. lemon juice
- 1 tsp. dried oregano
- salt and pepper
- water

Directions:

1. In a pot, boil water with salt over high heat. Add the penne once boiling to cook until tender. Drain.
2. Meanwhile, melt butter and sauté onions and garlic for about 2 minutes using a large skillet. Add the chicken and continue cooking for about 6 minutes tossing regularly.

3. Right before taking out of the skillet, add the artichoke, tomatoes, feta cheese, parsley, dried oregano, and lemon juice. Mix, toss in the penne and cook about 3 more minutes. Season with salt and ground black pepper. Serve warm.

Nutrition Facts:

Total calories 375, sodium 62 mg, total fat 12 g, carbs 46 g, saturated fat 2 g, dietary fiber 8 g, monounsaturated fat 5 g, protein 26 g, cholesterol 0 mg.

Classic Pasta Salad

Another classic pasta dish that's quintessentially Italian, try this recipe to boost your repertoire of healthy Mediterranean cuisines that are easy to prepare and good for your health.

Image credit: Jim Bathe

Yield: 4 servings

Best served for: Dinner

Ingredients:

- 1 cup multi-grain farfalle pasta
- 1 lemon, juiced, zest grated
- 2 tsp. olive oil
- 2 cups artichoke hearts, chopped
- 1 cup mozzarella

- cheese, chopped
- ¼ cup red bell pepper, chopped, roasted
- ¼ cup fresh parsley, chopped
- ½ cup peas

Directions:

1. To cook the pasta, follow the instructions indicated in the package.
2. As the pasta is cooking, prepare the dressing by mixing the lemon juice and zest with 2 teaspoons of olive oil in a large bowl. Slowly add the cheese, parsley, bell pepper and artichoke hearts and mix well.
3. Once the pasta is cooked, drain the water and add the peas. Toss to mix. Add the dressing to finish and serve while still warm.

Nutrition Facts:

Total calories 420, total fat 20g, saturated fat 8g, monounsaturated fat 2g, polyunsaturated fat 1g, protein 20g, carbs 50g, fiber 8g, cholesterol 45mg, sodium 200mg.

Potato salad, Mediterranean-Style

Anyone taking up the Mediterranean diet should have this simple and easy-to-prepare recipe in their arsenal; no questions asked!

ge credit: Goodfood.com

Yield: 4 servings

Best served for: Breakfast, dinner

Ingredients:

- 1 tbsp. olive oil
- 1 small onion, thinly sliced
- 1 garlic clove, crushed
- 1 tsp.

- oregano, fresh
- 200g cherry tomatoes
- 100g red peppers, roasted, sliced
- 300g small potatoes
- 25g black olives, sliced
- ¼ cup basil leaves, finely chopped

Directions:

1. In a medium-sized saucepan, heat the oil and add the onion to caramelize for about 3 to 5 minutes. Toss in the oregano, basil and garlic and cook for another 1 minute. Continue sautéing with the roasted pepper, olives and tomatoes for 10 minutes.
2. While sautéing, cook the potatoes in boiling water for about 10 minutes.
3. Finish by mixing the potatoes and sauce. Serve warm.

Nutrition Facts:

Total calories 110, protein 3g, carbs 16g, fat 4g, saturated fat 1g, fiber 2g, sugar 3g, salt 0.2g.

Couscous with Oil-Cured Olives

Couscous is a popular Greek and Israeli dish that's an excellent substitute for Western carb sources like rice, corn, or wheat. On top of more conventional healthy options like whole-grain bread or natural bran, you can now rely on couscous for your everyday carb requirements using this simple and filling recipe.

Yield: 4 servings

Best served for: Breakfast

Image credit: Allrecipe.com

Ingredients:

- ½ cup oil-cured black olives, chopped
- 2 tbsp. extra-virgin olive oil
- 3 cloves garlic, minced

- 1 yellow onion, minced
- 2 cups couscous, uncooked
- 3 ½ cups vegetable broth
- salt
- ½ cup walnuts, chopped, toasted

Directions:

1. Using a medium-sized saucepan, sauté garlic with olive oil for about 2 minutes stirring constantly. Add the onions to caramelize and continue cooking for about 2 minutes. Pour the couscous together and toss over medium heat until the couscous gains a golden brown color. Remember to stir constantly as the couscous can easily burn.

2. Add the vegetable broth and black olives and maintain medium heat to bring the mixture to a boil. Once boiling, reduce the heat to simmer and cook for another 15 until the liquid has reduced. Add the olives and salt to taste. Right before

taking out of the heat, toss in the walnuts to garnish. Serve warm.

Nutrition Facts:

Total calories 288, fat 10 g, saturated fat 1 g, monounsaturated fat 4 g, cholesterol 3 mg, sodium 229 mg, carbs 40 g, fiber 3 g, protein 9 g.

Roasted Vegetables in Balsamic Sauce

Roasting vegetables is not a common cooking strategy in Western cooking but in areas around the Mediterranean, it's frequently done for vegetables that are in-season. Here's one sample recipe that uses that technique to perfection to produce a dish that's light but very filling.

Image credit: Whatdidyoueat.typepad.com

Yield: 6 servings

Best served for: Dinner

Ingredients:

- 2 tbsp. balsamic vinegar
- 1 tsp. dijon mustard
- ½ cup extra-virgin olive oil
- 3 garlic cloves, crushed
- 2 tsp. thyme, finely chopped
- 1 tsp. basil, finely chopped
- 2 large red onions, thinly sliced
- 1 yellow, red, and orange bell pepper, each cut into strips
- 1 pound eggplant, quartered
- ½ pound yellow squash, cut into rounds
- 1 cup zucchini, cut into rounds
- salt and pepper

Directions:

1. To prepare the dressing, mix the balsamic vinegar and mustard in a bowl, then slowly add the olive oil. When mixed

properly, toss in the thyme, basil and garlic and season with pepper and salt.

2. To roast the vegetables, preheat oven to 450°F. Toss the onions, peppers, zucchini, squash and eggplant into a large bowl and season with salt and pepper. Pour the dressing to fully coat the vegetables. Lay down the veggies on a baking pan lined with a baking sheet. Roast for about 35 minutes until the edges brown.
3. Take out of the oven and pour the dressing, then serve warm.

Nutrition Facts:

Total calories 239, fat 19g, saturated fat 3g, sodium 32 mg, carbs 18 g, fiber 6 g, protein 3 g.

Artichokes Provencal

Here's a great way to take advantage of in-season artichokes. Enjoy!

Image credit: Whatdidyoueat.typepad.com

Yield: 4 servings

Best served for: Dinner

Ingredients:

- ½ onion, chopped
- 2 cloves garlic, chopped
- salt and pepper
- 1 tbsp. olive oil
- ½ cup white wine
- 2 tomatoes, chopped
- 2 cups

- artichokes, chopped
- water
- 1-strip lemon zest, to garnish
- ¼ cup olives, chopped
- ¼ cup basil, finely chopped

Directions:

1. Using a medium-sized skillet, sauté the onion, with the garlic. Add salt to taste. To the mixture, pour in the white wine and simmer until the liquid has reduced by about half. Then, add in the tomatoes, artichokes, together with about 3 tablespoons of water, and 1 strip of lemon zest to garnish. Continue seasoning with salt and pepper to taste. Cook for another 5 minutes. Stir the olives and basil to finish.
2. Serve warm.

Nutrition Facts:

Total calories 147, total fat 7.5g, saturated fat 1g, protein 4g, carbs 18g, sugar 5g, fiber 9g, cholesterol 0 mg, sodium 606 mg.

Tuscan-style white bean stew

Beans are a great source of protein, are very versatile ingredients that work for breakfast, lunch, dinner or even as a heavy-snack. Aside from having great flavor, the white bean stew is very popular because it's a stand-alone dish that can cater to one's nutritional needs any time of the year. This specific incarnation of the white bean stew can trace its roots to the Tuscan area of Italy and is particularly great during the fall and winter months when a filling warm soup without any meat becomes a prime commodity in communities around the Mediterranean.

Yield: 6 servings

Best served for: Dinner

Image credit: Picture Perfect Meals

Ingredients:

- 1 tbsp. extra-virgin olive oil
- ¼ tsp. black pepper, freshly ground
- 8 cloves garlic, minced
- 1 slice whole-grain bread, cut into cubes
- 2 cups dried white beans
- 6 cups water
- 1 tsp. salt
- 1 bay leaf
- 2 tbsp. olive oil
- 1 onion, chopped

- 3 carrots, peeled, chopped
- 2 cups vegetable stock
- 1 tbsp. fresh rosemary, chopped

Directions:

1. A night before cooking, soak the beans overnight to allow it to fluff up. In the morning, drain and rinse the beans and allow to sit for a couple of hours before cooking.
2. Using a pot, mix the white beans with water, salt and bay leaf and bring the mixture to a boil. Once boiling, reduce the heat and allow the soup to simmer for about 60 minutes until the beans are tender. Once cooked, drain the beans and reserve the liquid for later. Throw the bay leaf away.
3. To make the croutons, sauté 2 cloves of chopped garlic in a frying pan for about 1 minute. Take the pan out of the heat to allow the oil to absorb the flavors of the

garlic and allow to stand for about 10 minutes. Afterwards, remove the garlic and place the pan back on the heat. Now, add in the bread cubes and continue sautéing for about 5 minutes. Stir frequently to prevent from burning. Take the pan out of heat, transfer the contents on a bowl and set aside for later.
4. To make the stew, mix half a cup of water with half a cup of the cooked beans and mash into a paste. Add the paste into the remaining cooked beans.
5. Put the pot back into the heat and add some olive oil. Mix in the onion and carrots and sauté until the carrots are tender. Add the remaining 6 cloves of garlic, and continue sautéing. Season with salt, pepper, rosemary, and then add the bean mixture together with the vegetable stock. Boil the stew for about 5 minutes.
6. Serve hot with the croutons as garnish.

Nutrition Facts:

Total calories 328, sodium 450 mg, total fat 8 g, carbs 48 g, saturated fat1 g, dietary fiber 12 g, sugars 0 g, monounsaturated fat 6 g, protein 16 g, cholesterol 0 mg.

Chorizo pilaf

While the Mediterranean diet doesn't encourage regular consumption of meat, it never truly prohibits it either. In fact, there are big portions of Italy and Greece that pride themselves in cooking meat fresh from the local butcher. To ensure that the dish remains healthy, make sure you only use the freshest ingredients and not those from packaged products. This chorizo pilaf recipe is a great way to try and incorporate the meat into fresh local ingredients and is a superb way of breaking your "meat fast" once or twice a week.

Yield: 4 servings

Best served for: Dinner

Image credit: Goodfood.com

Ingredients:

- 1 tbsp. olive oil
- 1 large onion, thinly sliced
- 250g baby cooking chorizo, sliced
- 4 garlic cloves, crushed

- 1 tsp. paprika powder
- 12 pcs. plum tomatoes, chopped
- 250g basmati rice
- 4 cups vegetable stock
- 1 lemon, zest peeled, cut into wedges
- 2 fresh bay leaves
- ¼ cup parsley, chopped

Directions:

1. Heat the olive oil in a pan and sauté the onion for 5 minutes or until it turns soft and translucent. Add the chorizo and continue cooking until the meat gets a light brown color.

2. Next, add the garlic and paprika powder together with the tomatoes. Continue cooking for 5 minutes before adding the rice, vegetable stock, lemon zest and bay leaves. Stir until the stock boils, then turn down to low heat and allow to simmer for another 10 minutes.

3. Turn off the heat and finish by taking out the bay leaf and adding the parsley and squeezed lemon wedges.

Nutrition Facts:

Total calories 480, protein 19g, carbs 58g, fat 18g, saturates 6g, fiber 3g, sugar 9g, salt 1.4g.

Homemade Vegetable Pizza

Pizza, anyone? Now, you no longer need to call Dominoes if you want to enjoy a slice of pizza. Plus, because you can now cook your own, you can use only healthy ingredients to cut back on the unhealthy stuff. Yes, even pizza can be this simple!

Yield: 6 servings

Best served for: Dinner

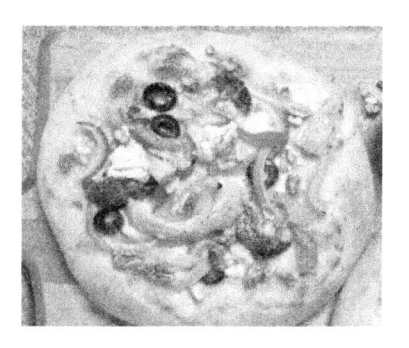

Image credit: walnuts.org

Ingredients:

- 1 cup water

- 2 tsp. active dry yeast
- pinch of sugar
- ½ tsp. salt
- 1 tbsp. olive oil
- 3 cups white flour (you can also mix it with whole wheat or rye flour)
- extra flour for kneading
- cornmeal

Various Toppings :

- cheese (mozzarella, parmesan, pecorino)
- red onions, thinly sliced
- mushroom, sliced
- bell pepper of different colors, sliced
- broccoli florets, torn
- artichoke hearts, sliced
- olives, pitted, sliced
- ripe tomatoes, sliced
- walnuts, chopped

Directions:

1. Activate the yeast by placing it in water together with the sugar. Allow it to stand for 5 minutes or until the water begins to bubble. Then, add in the salt, oil, and a cup of flour. Stir with a wooden spoon for several minutes to evenly mix the flour with the yeast. To finish the dough, gradually add the remaining flour half a cup at a time thoroughly mixing after each batch. The resulting dough should be soft but not sticky.

2. On a wooden surface, sprinkle flour and knead the dough for several minutes. Allow the dough to rest by placing in a bowl coated with oil. Cover it with plastic and set aside for one hour until the dough rises.

3. Now, you are ready to make the pizza. Split the dough into four balls and using the wooden surface, flatten each ball into the general shape of a pizza. On a baking tray sprinkled with cornmeal, place two dough circles each. Top each pizza with

any combination of ingredients that you like.

4. Preheat the oven to 500°F before putting in the pizza dough. Allow it to bake for about 12 minutes each. Serve hot.

Nutrition Facts:

Total calories 480, protein 19g, carbs 58g, fat 18g, saturates 6g, fiber 3g, sugar 9g, salt 1.4g.

Zucchini "Tagliatelle"

This zucchini salad is perfect for weight conscious diet enthusiasts who want a quick go-to recipe for breakfast, lunch or dinner. The salad can be easily prepared within 10 minutes and packed for the office. The salad also works well with any green smoothie of your choice as it can be easily spiced up with various flavors like lemon or mint. Lastly, add some nuts to this salad to boost its texture. It's definitely a salad that you will come to love for many more years to come!

Yield: 6 servings

Best served for: Dinner

Image credit: Citronetvanille.com

Ingredients:

- 1 large zucchini, peeled, seeded, diced
- 1 cup white onion, finely chopped
- 1 ½ cups fresh mint leaves, chopped
- 2 tsp. lemon peel, finely grated
- 4 tbsp. fresh lemon juice
- 2 tbsp. pistachio oil (or olive oil)
- salt and pepper

Directions:

1. Slice the zucchini into thin long strips. Do not include the core. To the zucchini, add the chopped onions, mint, and lemon peel. Flavor by adding the lemon juice and pistachio or olive oil. Season with salt and pepper.

2. Serve cold by refrigerating up to 3 hours before meal time.

Nutrition Facts:

Total calories 83, fat 5g, cholesterol 0 mg, sodium 15mg, carbs 9g, fiber 3g, protein 2g.

Spicy Escarole

This spicy escarole is perfect for those who want a little bit of kick in their salad. The escarole is also a great option in diversifying your selection of healthy greens.

Yield: 4 servings

Best served for: Breakfast, dinner

Image credit: Antonis Achilleos

Ingredients:

- 3 garlic cloves, minced
- olive oil
- pinch of red pepper flakes
- 1 head of escarole, torn

- salt and pepper

Directions:

1. Sauté the garlic in olive oil for about 2 minutes. Flavor with red pepper flakes before adding the escarole and then tossing in salt and pepper to taste. Cover and cook for about 5 minutes. Serve warm.

Nutrition Facts:

Total calories 74, fat 4g, cholesterol 0 mg, sodium 22mg, carbs 12g, fiber 5g, protein 1g.

Eggplant with Yogurt and Dill

Another simple salad made from cheap and readily available ingredients, this eggplant with yogurt and fill is a great fixer-upper prior to any morning rush.

Yield: 4 servings

Best served for: Breakfast

Anchilleos

Image credit: Antonis

Ingredients:

- 2 large eggplants, chopped
- 3 shallots, chopped
- 3 garlic

- cloves, crushed
- ¼ cup olive oil
- ½ cup walnuts, toasted
- ½ cup plain yogurt
- ½ cup fresh dill
- salt and pepper

Directions:

1. On a baking pan lined with a baking sheet, lay down the chopped eggplant together with the shallots and garlic. Sprinkle with olive oil, salt and pepper to flavor. Roast the ingredients for 30 minutes in a 400°F oven.
2. After 30 minutes, toss in the walnuts, and add the yogurt, dill and more salt and pepper to flavor. Serve hot.

Nutrition Facts:

Total calories 95, fat 7g, cholesterol 0 mg, sodium 35mg, carbs 16g, fiber 8g, protein 3g.

Braised Kale

Another fantastic way to enjoy kale, use this recipe if you bought a ton of kale in excess and want variety between meals. This recipe becomes even more alive with the addition of fresh cherry tomatoes and cooked in vegetable broth. Adding lemon juice as flavoring also brings another added layer to the taste of kale salad.

Yield: 4 servings

Best served for: Breakfast

Image credit: Myrecipes.com

Ingredients:

- 2 tsp. extra-virgin olive oil
- 4 garlic cloves, thinly sliced

- ½ white onion, chopped
- 4 cups kale, chopped
- ½ cup vegetable stock
- 1 cup cherry tomatoes, halved
- 1 tbsp. fresh lemon juice
- ¼ tsp. salt
- 1/8 tsp. black pepper, ground

Directions:

1. Sauté the garlic and onion in olive oil over medium heat until golden brown, then add the kale and vegetable stock and allow to boil and reduce. You know the kale is ready because it has wilted and now has a dark greenish color.
2. Add the tomatoes and continue cooking for 5 more minutes. Remove from the heat and flavor with lemon juice, salt and pepper. Serve hot.

Nutrition Facts:

Total calories 93, sodium 206 mg, total fat 3 g, carbs 15 g, saturated fat 0 g, dietary fiber 3 g, monounsaturated fat 2 g, protein 4 g, cholesterol 0 mg.

"For Adults Only" Mediterranean Chicken

This "for adults only" recipe brings together the combination of chicken with white wine. Of course, it's quintessentially Mediterranean flavors requires the addition of fresh and readily available produce that makes it one of the best ways to "cheat" with meat while still eating a healthy and filling meal.

Image credit: Allrecipes.com

Yield: 6 servings

Best served for: Breakfast

Ingredients:

- 2 tsp. olive oil
- 6 pcs. chicken breast, skinless, boneless
- 3 cloves garlic, minced
- ½ cup onion, diced
- 3 cups tomatoes, chopped
- 2/3 cup white wine
- 2 tsp. fresh thyme, chopped
- 1 tbsp. fresh basil, chopped
- ½ cup olives, chopped
- ¼ cup fresh parsley, chopped
- salt and pepper

Directions:

1. Sauté the chicken in 2 tablespoons of white wine over medium heat and cook for about 6 minutes on each side until the pinkish color disappears. Remove chicken from the heat and set aside.

2. In the same pan, add the olive oil and sauté the garlic for 30 seconds, then add the onion and continue cooking for another 3 minutes. Continue building the flavors by adding the tomatoes and allow the whole mixture to come to a boil. Once boiling, turn down the heat and toss in half a cup of white wine and simmer for another 10 minutes to reduce. Garnish with basil and thyme and continue simmering for 5 minutes.

3. To finish, toss in the chicken to the skillet and cook over low heat until the chicken is cooked through. Add the parsley and olives, salt and pepper, and toss for one more minute before taking out of the heat.

4. Serve hot.

Nutrition Facts:

Total calories 183, sodium 153 mg, total fat 15 g, carbs 22 g, saturated fat 2 g, dietary fiber 7 g, monounsaturated fat 5 g, protein 36 g, cholesterol 0 mg.

Tuna Salad Supreme

Every chef has to have a go-to tuna salad recipe. Make this one yours!

Yield: 6 servings

Best served for: Breakfast, afternoon snack

Image credit: Health.com

Ingredients:

- 2 cans tuna flakes, drained
- ¼ cup mayonnaise dressing
- ¼ cup olive oil
- ¼ cup red peppers, roasted, chopped
- ¼ cup olives, pitted, chopped

- 2 green onions, sliced
- 1 tbsp. small capers
- 6 slices whole wheat bread

Directions:

1. Mix all the ingredients in a bowl. Serve with the bread.

Nutrition Facts:

Total calories 190, fat 6g, saturated fat1g, protein18g, carbs 13g, fiber 2g, cholesterol 20mg, sodium 540mg.

Broccoli Rabe

Here's a great new way to enjoy your regular fix of broccoli! Make it a point to prepare this dish at least once a week!

Yield: 4 servings

Best served for: Breakfast, dinner

Image credit: Antonis Anchilleos

Ingredients:

- 2 bunches broccoli
- ¼ cup cherry peppers (in a jar, together with the liquid)
- 2 garlic cloves, sliced

- 1 tbsp. olive oil
- salt and pepper
- ¼ cup parmesan, grated

Directions:

1. Steam the broccoli in a standard steamer for about 8 minutes until tender.
2. In a separate pan, sauté garlic, peppers, and 2 tablespoons of the pepper liquid in the jar for about 3 minutes. Add the steamed broccoli and season with salt and pepper to taste. Finish by adding olive oil and top with shaved parmesan cheese.

Nutrition Facts:

Total calories 177, total fat 8 g, saturated fat 1 g, protein 12 g, carbs 17 g, sugar 4 g, fiber 0 g, cholesterol 0 mg, sodium 377 mg.

Classic Caponata

The caponata is a classic Italian eggplant recipe. While there are multiple variants, this one passionately appeals to your need to only eat vegetable ingredients. However, If you so choose, you can also experiment by copying the Palermo version by adding some squid or octopus to the recipe! The Sicilian version prefers to use lobster or local fishes in the area including swordfish and even shrimp. There is also a Neapolitan version known as the cianfotta.

Either way, this eggplant salad is sure to make your day!

In recent years, modern incarnations of the caponata have pegged it as a side dish for fish recipes but in olden times, this used to be a main course. We suggest you enjoy your caponata as a stand-alone dish that you can enjoy for breakfast or dinner.

Yield: 4 servings

Best served for: Breakfast, dinner

Image credit: Goodfood.com

Ingredients:

For the caponata:

- ½ cup extra-virgin olive oil
- 3 large eggplants, cut into cubes
- 2 shallots, chopped
- 4 plum tomatoes, chopped
- 2 tsp. capers, fresh
- ¼ cup raisins
- 4 celery sticks, sliced
- ½ cup red wine vinegar
- ½ cup pine nuts and basil leaves, toasted
- salt and pepper

For the bruschetta:

- 8 slices ciabatta bread
- olive oil
- 1 garlic clove, crushed
- salt

Directions:

1. To prepare the caponata, pour olive oil into a saucepan and put on medium heat. Add the eggplant and allow to cook for about 15 minutes until the vegetables are soft. Now, take the eggplants out of the pan and set aside for later.

2. On the same pan, add the shallots and cook for 5 minutes until they caramelize. Continue cooking by adding the tomatoes then put the eggplant back in. After about 2 minutes of continuous stirring, add the celery, capers, raisins, and red wine vinegar. Season to taste. Allow to simmer in low heat for about 35 minutes until all the vegetables are broken down into a soft mush.

3. Once cooked, turn off the heat to cool. You can now prepare the bruschetta. In a

griddled pan, wet the bread with olive oil and allow to toast for about 3 minutes. Season with more olive oil, salt, and garlic.
4. Top the caponata with pine nuts and basil leaves together with the bread.

Nutrition Facts:

Total calories 23, protein 4g, carbs 20g, fat 15g, saturated fat 2g, fiber 5g, sugar 8g, salt 0.4g.

Roasted Eggplant & Walnut Dip

If you prefer to enjoy your eggplants in ways other than the caponata, you can always try this roasted eggplant dish served with a flavorful walnut dip. You can also serve this with bread that you baked or bought at the local store. Various types of bread work well with the walnut dip but you can never go wrong with freshly baked pita bread.

Yield: 4 servings

Best served for: Morning or afternoon snack

Image credit: Walnuts.org

Ingredients:

- 1 large eggplant
- ½ cup walnuts, chopped
- 1 ½ tbsp. fresh mint, chopped
- 1 tbsp. fresh lemon juice
- 1 large clove garlic, minced
- 1 tsp. olive oil
- salt and pepper
- 4 pita bread
- 4 tbsp. parmesan, grated

Directions:

1. Pierce the eggplant with a fork to allow it to breathe while roasting. Then, wrap it in foil and pop into a 425°F oven for about 45 minutes until soft. Allow the eggplant to cool.

2. Once cool, split the roasted eggplant into two in the lengthwise direction and scrape the pulp out into a blender. Blend this and then set aside.

3. Using a saucepan over medium-high heat, toast the walnuts for about 2 minutes, then add the blended eggplant pulp. Flavor by adding garlic, olive oil, mint, and lemon juice. Season with salt and pepper.

4. Toast the pita bread for about 3 minutes in the oven. Once done, sprinkle with cheese while still hot. Serve the bread with the dip.

Nutrition Facts:

Total calories 40, total fat 2 g, saturated fat 0 g, monounsaturated fat 0 g, cholesterol 1 mg, sodium 45 mg, carbs 4 g, dietary fiber 1 g, protein 1 g.

Shrimp Skewers with Tzatziki and Feta Cheese

The recipe name says it all; shrimp on skewers served with tzatziki and feta cheese. That's about as decadent as you can ever get from a Mediterranean dish, and really this one will not disappoint! You can also serve this dish together with bread or pita chips to balance out the meal with healthy carbs.

Image credit: Sang An

Yield: 4 servings

Best served for: Dinner

Ingredients:

- 1 pound large shrimps, peeled, deveined, tails intact
- 1 cup yogurt, non-fat
- 1 cup cucumber, cut into cubes
- 3 tbsp. fresh dill, chopped
- 2 tbsp. fresh lemon juice

- 2 tbsp. chopped shallots
- 1 ¼ tsp. aniseed, finely crushed
- olive oil
- 8 cups baby spinach leaves
- ¾ cup feta cheese. Crumbled
- salt and pepper

Directions:

1. Prepare the tzatziki by mixing the yogurt with dill, cucumber, shallots and 2 tablespoons of lemon juice, plus ¾ teaspoon of crushed aniseed. Season with salt and pepper to the flavor you want and chill in the freezer for a few minutes. Note that it would be preferable, but not required, to use Greek yogurt for the tzatziki to get the proper consistency and flavor.

2. To cook the shrimps, skewer onto metal sticks and brush with olive oil, salt, pepper, and aniseed before grilling. Grill over medium heat until the shrimp turns reddish; this should not take more than 3 minutes. Be careful not to overcook the shrimp.

3. To plate, use the spinach as a base and drizzle with olive oil and lemon juice.

Place one skewer in each plate and a dollop of tzatziki and feta cheese.

Nutrition Facts:

Total calories 289 kcal, fat 11.50g, saturated fat 5.40g, cholesterol 0.25g, carbs 14g, dietary fiber 3g, sugars 6g, protein 33g.

Bulgur Salad

Bulgur is a type of wheat, often taken from the durum variety, and is a great alternative to conventional sources of carbs in your diet. This bulgur salad is one great example of how you can add bulgur to your Mediterranean diet with a very simple but great recipe. You also have the freedom to choose the vegetable toppings that you want to enjoy with the bulgur so go ahead and experiment with your flavor preferences.

Yield: 6 servings

Best served for: Breakfast, light dinner

Image credit: Tina Rup

Ingredients:

- 2 cups bulgur, uncooked
- 2 tbsp. butter
- 4 tbsp. olive oil
- 4 cups water
- salt
- ½ cucumber, seedless, chopped
- 2 tsp. red wine vinegar
- ¼ cup fresh dill, chopped
- ¼ cup black olives, pitted, chopped

Directions:

1. Cook the bulgur by tossing it into a pan together with olive oil and butter. As a rule of thumb, 2 cups of bulgur require about 2 tablespoons each of butter and olive oil. You know the bulgur is ready when it has developed a lightly golden brown color.
2. Add in about 4 cups water and flavor with season with salt. Allow to simmer until the liquid has reduced and the bulgur is soft and tender. This should take not more than 15 to 20 minutes.

3. Top the bulgur with cucumber chunks flavored with red wine vinegar, dill, olive oil, and black olives.

Nutrition Facts:

Total calories 386, total fat 17 g, saturated fat 5 g, protein 9 g, carbs 55 g, sugar 1 g, fiber 13 g, cholesterol 15 mg, sodium 229 mg.

Poached Pear in Orange and Apple Juice

Fruits aren't just good for eating raw. Some of them, like pears for example, are also great when carefully cooked and properly flavored. Tis poached pear recipe will show you that it doesn't take a chef to prepare a great dinner from just the simplest of ingredients in your kitchen. Enjoy!

Yield: 4 servings

Best served for: Dessert

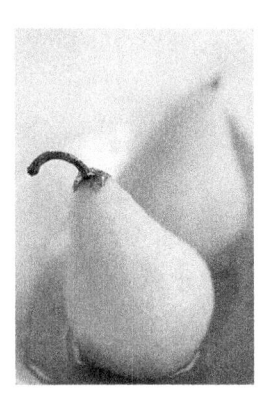

Image credit: Simplyrecipes.com

Ingredients:

- 1 cup orange juice
- ¼ cup apple juice
- 1 tsp. cinnamon, ground

- 1 tsp. nutmeg, ground
- 4 whole pears
- ½ cup fresh raspberries
- 2 tbsp. orange zest

Directions:

1. In a bowl, mix the apple juice and orange juice with the cinnamon and nutmeg. Stir well.

2. Carefully peel the pears but leave the stem at the top. Also core the pear from the bottom so the hole doesn't show when the pear is sitting upright. Now, place the pear in a pan and pour in the juices, making sure that the pears are floating in the juice and not touching the bottom of the pan. Cook over medium heat and simmer for about 30 minutes. Always check that the mixture doesn't boil.

3. To finish, garnish the pear with raspberries and orange zest. Serve immediately while the pear is still hot.

Nutrition Facts:

Total calories 145, sodium 0 mg, total fat 0 g, carbs 36 g, saturated fat 0 g, dietary fiber 5 g, monounsaturated fat 0 g, protein 1 g, cholesterol 0 mg.

Avocado and Tuna Tapas

Tapas are Spain's equivalent of finger foods or cocktail foods. These are great for any occasion and can be easily prepare at a moment's notice. This version takes advantage of the complementary flavors of tuna and avocado when prepared properly. Enjoy!

Yield: 4 servings

Best served for: Dessert

Image credit: Allrecipes.com

Ingredients:

- 1 ½ cup white tuna
- 1 tbsp. mayonnaise
- 3 green onions, thinly sliced
- ½ red bell pepper, chopped
- 2 tbsp. balsamic vinegar
- 1 pinch salt and black pepper
- 2 ripe avocados, halved, pitted

Directions:

1. In a bowl, mix the tuna, with green onions, red pepper, mayonnaise, and balsamic vinegar. Season with salt and pepper.
2. Garnish the mixture on top of the avocado as in the picture above. Finish with green onions and a dash of black pepper on top before serving.

Nutrition Facts:

Total calories 161, sodium 36 mg, total fat 10 g, carbs 24 g, saturated fat 2 g, dietary fiber 5 g, monounsaturated fat 4 g, protein 1 g, cholesterol 0 mg.

Mediterranean-Style Chickpea Patties

Chickpea patties are great alternatives to meat slices. These are actually very common in vegan and vegetarian cooking and those on a Mediterranean diet can benefit from this as well. Try out this simple but elegant Mediterranean-style recipe so you can eventually include this in the regular list of dishes you cook for you and your family.

Yield: 4 servings

Best served for: Breakfast, lunch, afternoon snack, dinner

Image credit: Hallie Burton

Ingredients:

- 2 cups chickpeas
- ½ cup fresh flat-leaf parsley

- 1 garlic clove, chopped
- ¼ tsp. cumin, ground
- ½ tsp. salt
- ½ tsp. black pepper
- 1 egg, whisked
- 4 tbsp. flour
- 2 tbsp. olive oil
- ½ cup low-fat yogurt
- 3 tbsp. fresh lemon juice
- 8 cups mixed salad greens
- 1 cup grape tomatoes, halved
- ½ small red onion, thinly sliced

Directions:

1. Use a blender or food processor to combine the chickpeas, parsley, garlic and cumin and flavor with salt and pepper. Transfer the mixture to a bowl and whisk the egg together with 2 tablespoons flour. Use the resulting dough to form 8 patties, each about half an inch thick. Afterwards, roll all the patties in the remaining flour and dust off.

2. To fry the dough, use a nonstick skillet over medium heat. Pour in olive oil and cook the patties for about 3 minutes on each side or until golden brown.

3. Prepare the dip by combining yogurt, lemon juice, salt and pepper. Plate the greens, tomatoes, and onion as a bed on each serving plate. Put two patties in

each plate and add a dollop of the dressing.

Nutrition Facts:

Total calories 225, fat 8g, saturated fat 1g, monounsaturated fat 4g, polyunsaturated fat 2g, protein 12g, carbs 29g, fiber 8g, cholesterol 54mg, iron 4mg, sodium 387mg, calcium 136mg.

Chili Spinach Salad

Had enough with kale? Try this spinach salad instead. This recipe closely resembles the spicy escarole recipe earlier with a few simple twists. If you want a simple-to-prepare but filling dish that you can eat for lunch or dinner, and provided you don't mind the kick of extra spice on your food, then this is definitely the recipe for you.

Yield: 4 servings

Best served for: Lunch, dinner

Image credit: Goodfood.com

Ingredients:

- 25g butter
- 1 cup fresh breadcrumbs
- 1 lemon zest, grated
- 2 garlic cloves, crushed
- 1 red chili, finely chopped
- 3 cups spinach, coarsely chopped

Directions:

1. Melt the butter in a pan, then add the garlic, chili, zest and breadcrumbs. Cook until the crumbs turn golden. Season with

a little bit of salt. Set the breadcrumbs aside.

2. In the same pan, toss the spinach for about 5 minutes and season to taste. Take out of heat and top with the breadcrumbs.

Nutrition Facts:

Total calories 169, protein 7g, carbs 20g, fat 7g, saturated fat 3g, fiber 3g, sugar 3g, salt 1g.

Mediterranean-style scones

Image credit: Goodfood.com

Scones; really, need we say more? Try this scones recipe so you have the perfect home-baked bread to complement your other Mediterranean dishes. Scones work well as accompaniment to salads or as appetizer before a main dish; either way, your homemade scones should be house-favorites from the very first day you learn to bake these marvelous golden-brown delicacies.

Yield: 8 servings

Best served for: All meals

Ingredients:

- 3 cups self-rising flour
- 1 tbsp. baking powder
- ¼ tsp. salt
- 1 stick butter, cut in pieces
- 1 tbsp. olive oil
- 8 halves sundried tomatoes, chopped

- 100g feta cheese, cubed
- 10 black olives, pitted, halved
- 2 cups full fat milk
- 1 egg, beaten

Directions:

1. Preheat the oven to 220°C. Also, prepare the baking pan by lining it with baking sheet coated in butter.

2. To prepare the dough, mix the flour, salt and baking powder thoroughly. Add 2 teaspoons of olive oil, then the butter until the dough adopts the consistency of fine crumbs. Finish the dough by adding the cheese, tomatoes and olives. Continue kneading the dough by shaping it into a "well" with a hole in the middle where you will pour the milk into. With a little more kneading, the resulting dough will then adopt a sticky consistency. The dough is now ready.

3. To make the scones, take 4-cm size balls from the dough until you have 8 scones in total. Brush each ball with the beaten egg and pop into the oven for about 20 minutes until it rises and has a golden brown color. Take out of the oven to cool.

4. Serve the scones warm and with butter.

Nutrition Facts:

Total calories 29, protein 8g, carbs 36g, fat 14g, saturated fat 7g, dietary fiber 2g, sugar 0g, salt 2g.

Mediterranean Veggie Wrap

The last recipe on our list is a healthy breakfast warp, just what you need to start the day right.

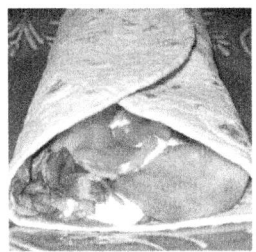

Image credit: Allrecipes.com

Yield: 4 servings

Best served for: Breakfast

Ingredients:

- 1 red onion, sliced
- 1 zucchini, sliced
- 1 eggplant, sliced
- ¼ pound fresh

- mushrooms, sliced
- 1 red bell pepper, sliced
- 1 tbsp. olive oil
- salt and ground black pepper
- 4 whole grain tortillas
- ¼ cup goat cheese
- ¼ cup basil pesto
- 1 large avocado, sliced

Directions:

1. Mix together the zucchini, eggplant, mushrooms, bell pepper and onion in one container and add olive oil. Mix thoroughly and season with salt and pepper.

2. Using a griddled pan over medium heat, cook the vegetable mix for about 10 minutes. Stir regularly to prevent burning.

3. Spread each tortilla with goat cheese and 1 tablespoon pesto. Pour the vegetables into each tortilla in equal portions. Fold to serve.

Nutrition Facts:

Total calories 85, protein 5g, carbs 45g, fat 8g, saturated fat 2g, dietary fiber 6g, sugar 0g, salt 4g.

A Sample 7-Day Mediterranean Diet for Transitioning into Healthy Eating

Here is a sample 7-day Mediterranean diet using some of the recipes we just outlined. Try this out if you want to begin a lifestyle relying mostly on the Mediterranean diet for nutrition in order to achieve your health goals for the coming year.

Day	Breakfast	Lunch	Dinner
1	Mediterranean-Style Quinoa salad	Sicilian-Style Cauliflower Salad	Chicken and penne
2	Pita Sandwiches stuffed with Greek salad	Mediterranean Kale Salad with roasted grape vinaigrette	Pasta with Basil-Based Sauce
3	Greek Salad with Orzo and black-eyed peas	Zucchini "Tagliatelle"	Balsamic Chicken and Mediterranean Salad
4	Couscous with oil-cured olives	Roasted Mediterranean vegetables with polenta	Mint-Flavored Grilled Lamb chops

5	Potato salad, Mediterranean-style	Greek Salad	Chorizo pilaf
6	Walnut Granola Cereals	Tuna Salad Supreme	Grilled salmon
7	Mediterranean-Style Panini	Artichokes Provencal	Roasted vegetables in balsamic sauce

Conclusion

The Mediterranean diet is an easy and practical way to help you achieve your health and weight goals without fooling like you are starving yourself to death. And because the cooking style is fairly easy and the ingredients readily available, you can be confident enough to prepare your own delicious meals every day.

We also recommend that you pick up the accompanying ebook "The Mediterranean Diet: Modern Healthy Eating and What It Can Do for You" to help you better understand the Mediterranean Diet as your ticket to better health. Armed with these two ebooks, you know you are well informed and on your way towards finally having the body that you want and deserve!